~ pictures & postcards from the past

Cheadle Hulme

Morris Garratt

Published by Sigma Leisure – an imprint of
Sigma Press, 1 South Oak Lane, Wilmslow, Cheshire SK9 6AR, England.

British Library Cataloguing in Publication Data
A CIP record for this book is available from the British Library.

ISBN: 1-85058-674-8

Typesetting and Design by: Sigma Press, Wilmslow, Cheshire.

Cover: this picture postcard was used for many towns in the early 1900s – Cheadle Hulme was not unique in its romantic interludes!

Printed by: MFP Design and Print

Acknowledgements

It is a pleasure to record my thanks to the following individuals and organisations that have most generously made their photographs available to me, or have given help with information. It will be apparent from the following list that this book has been compiled and has been waiting for publication over a long period. I am saddened that some contributors did not live to see their photographs in print, and I am also grateful to everyone for their forbearance in not pressing for the return of their material before publication could be achieved.

The late Frank and Teretta Mitchell; Mr. W. Green; Mr. B.J. Thompson; Mr. J.P. Harrison; Mr. A.F. Hiney; Mr.B. Jeuda; Mrs. Carol Squire; Mrs. E.B.Waine; The late Mr. F.Heusel; The late Mr. W.J. Skillern and Mr. P.W. Skillern; Mr. S. Madders and Mr.H.E. Madders; Mrs. Whittaker, teacher, and Mr.D. Pennells, headteacher, both from the former Cheadle Hulme High School; Mr.D.Goodison, formerly of Cheadle Hulme School; Past and present members of the staff of the Stockport Local Heritage Library (formerly the Library of Local Studies); Rev. N.Brunning and Rev.S.Foster, previous incumbents of All Saints Parish Church; Mr. I. Miller. My thanks also to Mr. D. Seddon not only for providing material but also for copying some of the old photographs and obtaining remarkable results. Finally, and in the hope that I have not overlooked anyone, my thanks to my wife Eileen for her encouragement, support and assistance - and the coffee!

Dedication

To my wife Eileen, and Katherine, David and Richard, who have waited long and patiently for this book.

Morris Garratt

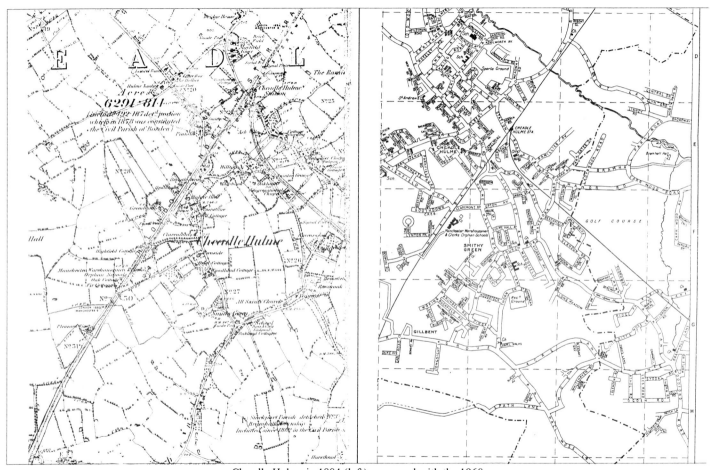

Cheadle Hulme in 1884 (left) compared with the 1960s

Introduction

There is no history in Cheadle Hulme - it's all just modern houses "and shops". So began one of the late Frank Mitchell's local history articles with that quotation from a student who turned up on his doorstep. But it hasn't always been like that, as you will see from some of the photographs assembled here. Cheadle Hulme, in fact, has indeed had an industrial past. The beginning of 'modern' Cheadle Hulme could perhaps be said to date from 1773 when a local mill owner advertised for velveret weavers, carders, rovers, spinners and cutters, and said he had homes to let "fit for families". Four years later the mill had two carding engines, five spinning jennies and a twisting jenny. Nearby were five houses "with room to contain ten looms".

At the time of the 1811 census the population of Cheadle Moseley (as the area was then called) is given as 1296, and this increased 50% by 1831. In 1811, 62 persons were employed in agriculture while 179 were in manufacturing. The textile connection remained throughout the nineteenth century: the individual hamlets which later merged into the Cheadle Hulme of today - such as Smithy Green, Grove Lane or Lane End - were centres for the domestic textile trade. In many cottages the handloom weaver could be heard, for Cheadle Hulme had a reputation of weaving silk by this method. Agriculture was another prominent local occupation: in the 1850s there were some 36 farms operating, and 22 still remained in 1887.

Perhaps the major single influence on the development of the area - as in many other places - was the coming of the railway, bringing as it did the Manchester (and for us, Stockport) businessmen and their families. Many of their large Victorian and Edwardian houses, for example in Swann Lane, Cheadle Road and Albert Road, still remain though in many cases now converted into flats.

In 1901, a writer on Cheadle Hulme included these words: "Cheadle Hulme, as we all know, is a very scattered district, there is no nucleus of a village with its village green and its high street; had there been an old church, there would no doubt have been a cluster of houses, with perhaps a few public houses, but until quite recently there has been no concentration of building, no definite plan, and in time the wants of the community are supplied by enterprising tradesmen. There is no difficulty in distinguishing between old and modern Cheadle Hulme, the old weavers' cottages, the farm house and the brick timber and thatched barns are so different from the modern structure that they proclaim themselves the landmarks of a past age, and appeal to us for the respect due to antiquity".

The developments of the 1930s and even more particularly the rapid changes since the last war have dramatically altered the face of Cheadle Hulme. In 1961, an article in the *Manchester Evening News* said: "In a short lifetime, vast changes have transformed the once sleepy hamlet of Cheadle Hulme into sophisticated suburbia".
Sophisticated suburbia - I like it!

Author's Note

I have provided rather more extensive notes to the photographs than is usual in publications of this kind, in the hope that the book will serve not only as a photographic record but also as a short history of Cheadle Hulme. Some changes in road names are mentioned in the main text; here are some others:

Ack Lane also appears as Hack Lane, Halk Lane and Oak Lane.

Acre lane may be a corruption of Acorn Lane.

Albert Road was formerly Stockport Road or Lane Ends; the new name commemorates the visit of Prince Albert to Abney Hall prior to the opening of the Art Treasures Exhibition held at Old Trafford, Manchester in 1857.

Cheadle Road was previously Street Lane, perhaps indicating some pre-historic or Roman origin.

Park Road is the new name for Hulme's Common Road.

Station Road was formerly called Cheadle Hulme Common Road.

Turves Road comes from Turves or Turf Lane.

1. Station Road Junction

One of the busiest junctions for motor traffic today, and especially during the morning and evening rush hours, is the meeting of Station Road, Ladybridge Road, Queens Road and Albert Road. Formerly known as Four Lane Ends, it was improved in 1961, but fifty or more years ago there was time for these two cyclists to stop for a chat in more peaceful surroundings. The way to Cheadle and Manchester is by Albert Road (to the right) with Station Road straight ahead. Today the shopping precinct and its large car park have replaced the trees behind our cyclists. The photograph is from a postcard sent in July 1941 by Rachel to "Dear Mummie" at Eccleston near Chorley, Lancashire.

2. Station Road

Station Road has always been the principal shopping district, and while there has been little change in the buildings, these two photographs show how road transport has developed. In the late 1920s the horse was still to be seen, but not so in the next photograph.

Station Road,
Cheadle Hulme

3. Station Road

Forty years later and the car has taken over. Common to both views are the premises of Messrs Pimlott, who established their business next to the railway station in 1869.

Station Rd., Cheadle Hulme.

4. Station Road - King's Hall

The year 1937 was noteworthy nationally for the Coronation of King George VI and Queen Elizabeth, but here in Cheadle Hulme it also marked the building of the King's Hall, which quickly became the venue for local societies. During the 1939-45 war, the Hall was used by the local Roman Catholic community for Mass before they built their own church in Vicarage Avenue in 1952.

STATION ROAD, CHEADLE HULME.

G.8167.

5. Station Road, approximately 1945

The trees in the previous illustration hid the row of shops beyond Central Buildings. The taller structure with the conspicuous roofline is the *Elysian Cinema*, which opened on Saturday, 22 November 1930.

STATION ROAD, CHEADLE HULME

6. Station Road, 1974

This picture shows several changes from the previous one, which dated from *c.*1945. The cinema, its awning projecting over the pavement, had closed on 2 March 1974 (the picture was taken shortly afterwards) and is up for sale; it eventually became a supermarket.

7. Mellor Road

We see here how Mellor Road and its associated shopping facilities are situated between the junction of the railway lines to Macclesfield (to the left) and Crewe (to the right). Beyond Williams Deacon's Bank is Burgon's Ltd., grocers and provision merchants, with what appear to be a group of people on the balcony above the shop window. Next to Burgon's is the shop belonging to J. Waterhouse.

8. Waterhouse's shop, Mellor Road

This view dates from *c.* 1925. The business of J. Waterhouse, "fish, game and poultry dealer, English and foreign fruiterer", was established in 1921.

Cheadle Holme at Station

9. Waterhouse's Van

Mellor Road was originally called Mellor Street, as may be seen in this photograph of a Waterhouse delivery van, *c.*1930.

10. T. Jackson, Mellor Road

This photograph is something of an enigma. There appears to be a distinct similarity between Jackson's shop, shown here in a photograph said to date from around 1902, and Waterhouse's shop (see no.8). In the 'Commercial' section of an 1883 directory, Thomas Jackson, described as a grocer, was said to be in Market Street: could this be an error for Mellor Street? That same directory, under 'Private Residents', lists Thomas

Jackson, now described as a provision merchant, as living at Park House, Bramhall Lane, Cheadle Hulme. In 1887 he is a grocer again! In the 1892 directory he has gone to live in Cheadle Road, and he is not listed at all in 1902, so perhaps the photograph actually dates from some time before 1892? Whatever the truth may be, it's an interesting photograph nonetheless. Could it be that Mr. Waterhouse eventually purchased this shop in 1921 to start his business?

11. Cyclists, Grove Lane

Cycling, whether for pleasure or competition, was clearly a popular activity (see also pictures 72-74). Here, about 1898, we have Minnie Hooley, with Elizabeth, Fred and Harry Brunt, all from the Grove Lane area. Grove Lane, incidentally, used to be called Rogues Lane! "Grove Lane, which is now [1902] a very well behaved settlement of decent people, was in the memory of many people living a hotbed of vice, the abode of poachers and disreputable characters".

12. Fritz Koenen

Fritz Koenen seen outside the *Church Inn* in 1897 after his victory in a fifty-mile cycle race at a meeting with Cheadle Cycling Club.

13. Jonathan Robinson School

The first school in the area was provided by Jonathan Robinson, a Stockport merchant though born in Cheadle Hulme. In 1785, he gave three acres of land (Cheshire measure) on which to build a school for 14 pupils. The profits from the land, on the corner of Church Road and Woods lane, were to pay for a schoolmaster to instruct eight poor children, the other six being required to pay twopence [1p] per week.

The original plaque, visible in the photograph between the upper-storey windows, records that 'This school was built by subscription and endowed by Jonathan Robinson 1785'. It can now be seen in the present Cheadle Hulme College (formerly Cheadle Hulme High School), Woods Lane and was unveiled in its new position on 28 April 1986. The original school was enlarged in 1893 to form a public elementary school for 200 children, who transferred to the Church (National) school at age seven. The 1881 census records John Hindley and his wife Louise as Certificated Elementary Teachers; he came from Leigh and was then aged 42, while she was from Gloucester: they were still here in 1892.

Jonathan Robinson's signature is shown below:

Jon^a Robinson

14. All Saints (National) School

The National School, Church Road, Smithy Green - to give it its full address- was opened in 1873 as a result of the 1870 Education Act. It was built on the site of a farm previously occupied by the Faulkner family. The school became the venue for various church organisations until the Parish Hall opened in 1910. The school was demolished in 1973; the site is now occupied by All Saints Church Hall (opened in 1974) and a small car park. The first master was Elijah Chambers with Elizabeth Chambers as the first mistress.

15. All Saints (National) School

This photograph, dating from around 1904, shows the Headmaster, Alfred Boyd, and some of his young gentlemen. It looks as though they have been constructing a garden and pathway at some private property, though I cannot say where. Perhaps at the school? As with other photographs showing schoolchildren in this collection, the variety in the pupils' dress repays detailed study. Mr. Boyd's wife was mistress of the infants department.

16. All Saints (National) School

We see here a class photograph dated to 1913-14. So far, the following pupils have been identified: Back row: 1 - C.G. Kirk (Headmaster), 2 - Harry Hope, 3 - ?, 4 -? Stonehewer, 5 - ?, 6 -? Ada Burgess, 7 - Rose Lee, 8 -? Simcock, 9 - Iris Davies, 10 - Miss A. Leather (teacher). Third row: 1 - ?, 2 - E.Stansfield, 3 - ?, 4 - Ida Boulderstone (?), 5 -? Lena Davies, 6 - Effie Hall, 7 - ?, 8 - Lily Leather. Second row: 1 - Joe Burrows, 2 - ?, 3 -Maggie Cook, 4 - Marjorie Stewall, 5 - Kitty Grice, 6 - R.Williams, 7 - ? Markham, 8 - Edith Bratt, 9 - ? Feather, 10 - John Mitchell. Front row: 1 - Eric Green, 2 - ?, 3 - ?, 4 -F.Stokes(?), 5 - ? Pinnington, 6 - ?, 7 - ?, 8 - ?, 9 - ?.

17. Warehousemen and Clerks' Orphan School

The Manchester Warehousemen and Clerks' Orphan School, now an independent day and boarding school popularly known as Cheadle Hulme School, began modestly in 1855 with six children boarded out and educated at the Shaw Hall Academy at Flixton; by 1869, there were 19 children. In 1861 two houses were taken at Park Lane, Ardwick Green, for 23 children. The foundation stone at Cheadle Hulme was laid by Lord

Granville on 28 August 1867, and the school was opened by Lord Ellesmere on Saturday, 7 August 1869. A contemporary report described it as "3 storeys, brick faced with stone ...a plain substantial structure...neatly finished, without any display of ornament". There was accommodation for 130 children, but it then only had 50; 34 boys and 16 girls. The original building was by Ernest Bates; two wings were later added, in 1869 and 1903. In these early years, a typical day was: up at 6.30 a.m.; prep. till breakfast at 8; classes 9 a.m. to 12 noon and 2 p.m. to 4 p.m.; prep. again between 6.15 p.m. and 8.15 p.m. then promptly to bed at 8.30 p.m.

18. Warehousemen and Clerks' Orphan School

A selection of the girls, with only a few smiling faces, pictured in 1895 outside the school.

19. Warehousemen and Clerks' Orphan School
The School of Cookery, from the 1913-14 annual report.

20. Warehousemen and Clerks' Orphan School
The sixth-form classroom, also taken from the 1913-14 annual report.

21. Cheadle Hulme Station

The Stockport to Sandbach section of the Manchester and Birmingham Railway opened on 10 May 1842. Cheadle Hulme's first station was situated opposite the *Hesketh Arms* and was called Cheadle. This original station "consisted of a kind of sentry box, where a man attended to sell tickets, and stopped trains by signal, on dark nights lighting a candle as the signal in his cabin window". The original station house (though not the cabin or sentry box) still stands and is best seen from Heathbank Road.

This aerial view of the station dates from 1926. A prominent feature is the footbridge, which survived until the line was electrified. The station was used by Lord Vernon to distribute coal from his collieries at Poynton; the extensive goods yard is now - inevitably - a car park. Notice also the relatively rural appearance of the area.

22. Cheadle Hulme Station

It's about 1908 and these Edwardian ladies and gentlemen have just alighted from a southbound train on the main line (the lines seen disappearing under the 'Platform 2' sign are for Macclesfield). Who they are, and what the social occasion is, I would love to know! Not, I think, your average commuters! Apart from the various advertisements, notice also the platform seat with the station name on it.

23. Cheadle Hulme Station
Being on the main Manchester-Crewe-London line, Cheadle Hulme saw the transition from steam power to the latest electric and diesel locomotives earlier than some other local suburban stations. Here, in the days of steam, class 4F, no.44069 takes a freight train on to the Macclesfield line on 7 June 1951.

24. Cheadle Hulme Station
Five years later, on 19 July 1956, to be precise, and a new diesel train on a driver-training run from Macclesfield arrives at Cheadle Hulme, a few months before regular public services began.

25 & 26. Derailment

On 28 May 1964 a special train taking schoolchildren from Staffordshire to York was derailed at Cheadle Hulme while negotiating the curve on to the main line. Three people were killed. In the upper photograph, we see part of the train and the damaged platform. In the lower picture, the rear of the train is seen on the narrow bridge over Station Road.

27. Th old railway bridge

The original bridges and the narrowness of the road are seen in this view dating from about 1905. The bridge in the foreground carries the main line to London.

28. New bridge

Following the accident the station was modernised and new bridges erected. Sunday, 11 July 1965, and work is in progress on the new main line bridge. Notice the footbridge (top right-hand corner) with Mellor Road at the bottom left-hand corner.

29. Station entrance

This view of the station entrance is taken from Mellor Road and may be dated to 1937 or 1938. The Tudor Cinema, Bramhall, whose publicity appears on the hoarding, was opened on 31 March 1935 (it closed in 1958). The film *Talk of the Devil,* produced in 1936 and directed by Carol Reed, was the first film shot at Pinewood Studios. *The Frog* came out in 1937 and was produced by Herbert Wilcox.

30. Bus services

Omnibus services were also important in the growing village's development and were operated by the North Western Road Car Company. JA 5551 (NWRCC no.751) was one of three Dennis Lancet IIs purchased in 1936 and is seen here in Station Road on a local service about 1950. It was withdrawn in 1952.

31. Burslem's

In its issue dated 13 March 1857, *The Engineer* reported that a patent had been recorded on 17 February in the name of William and John Burslem of Cheadle, Cheshire, for "an improved 'picker' to be used in power looms for weaving". In the same year, *Kelly's Directory* lists Randle Burslem, of Cheadle Heath, as a stonemason. By 1860, the Free School at Cheadle Heath, disused for many years, had been occupied by Mr. W. Burslem as a patent picker manufactory - double box pickers for all kinds of shuttle looms. In 1864, John Burslem was the Parish Clerk at Cheadle. By 1872, William was living at Yew Tree Cottages, presumably in retirement.

The 1871 census lists Alexander Burslem, aged 36, as a brick-maker. He came from Stock-port, but his wife Sarah was born in Maryland in the United States. *Kelly's Directory* (1878) has Charles Frederick Burslem as a tanner spider maker and Alexander as a master brickmaker at Adswood. In the photograph, dating from about 1910, the man on the right is Thomas Burslem; the family brickworks was in the Tenement Lane area. The steam lorry had oil lamps, was chain driven on the rear wheels, and had a hose at the back for taking water from the public mains.

32. Millington Hall, *c.*1890

Millington Hall, on Station Road, is now a restaurant, but it was formerly the home of Alderman John Millington of Stockport and his wife Sarah. It dates from about 1683. Alderman Millington died on 1 September 1694 aged 54 and is buried at Cheadle. The name for this part of Cheadle Hulme in times past was Lane End, a name perpetuated in a local school. The Methodists had a Sunday School and Meeting Place at Lane End from December 1814; this was in a third-storey room in the row of cottages near to Millington Hall. This 'upper room' was reached by a flight of stairs through the second storey; inside was an oak beam of the natural shape of the tree, which served as a desk or pulpit. In 1815 there were 180 scholars. The cottages slightly pre-date the Hall, for the Millingtons lived there while their Hall was being built.

33. Silk handloom weaver

The weaving of silk by handloom was very common in parts of Cheadle Hulme in the last century and did not finally disappear until the early part of the present century. This particular photograph was taken about 1895, in an upper room at the rear of the Hall; the weaver may be a member of the Hazeldine family who lived at the Hall at that time. The wheel was used for winding the yarn and was still preserved at the Hall as late as 1976.

34. Dr. Knott

Dr. Thomas Brideoak Knott was born at Bolton in 1826 and in December 1864 was appointed Certifying Surgeon for Middleton and District by the Inspector of Factories for the Oldham Board of Guardians. The Public Health Act 1872 made the appointment of a Medical Officer of Health compulsory, and in the following year, Dr. Knott became the first Medical Officer of Health for Middleton, a post he held until his resignation in September 1880. In 1886, he was a founding member of the Cheadle and Gatley Local Board of Health. He died in 1911 and was buried at All Saints Parish Church, to whom he had given the eagle lectern in 1899.

The photograph is obviously one of a pair, for in a note to Dr.Knott on the reverse of the original, the unknown photographer has written: "On both of these the pony only seems to have 3 legs. I have not sent the other as there is no difference".

35. 'Ellerslie', Beechfield Road
The house, seen to better advantage in this photograph, still stands; it was called 'Ellerslie' in Dr. Knott's time and was later re-named 'Woodcote'.

36. Congregational Church, Swan Lane

The Congregationalists built their school before their church. The school was completed in May 1869 and the first services were held there on Sunday, 20 June. The Memorial Stone for the church had been laid on Tuesday, 27 May 1869 by Sir James Watts of Abney Hall; it was ready for use in the following year. The first services were held on Thursday, 7 July 1870, the preacher being the Rev. Thomas Binney of London. The architect, Henry Littler, who lived at Lane End, Cheadle Hulme, was aged 52 in 1881 and came from Sheffield. He had been asked to design a

chapel and schools, in stone, at a cost not to exceed £2000; the final cost, including furniture and fittings, was £3875-6s-8d. A feature of the church, and a distinctive local landmark, was the spire. Seen here in a photograph dating from c.1905, it was reduced in height in 1961. The church was burned down on 28 December 1977 and demolished the following year, to be replaced by the present smaller and modern building on the same site in 1979.

37. Congregational Church
The church provided a number of social activities; here we see a 'mock banquet' on Dickens Night in 1929.

38. The Rev. Griffith David Hughes
Rev. Hughes was minister from 1884-1901.

39. Ravenoak Road

It is perhaps difficult to imagine that the 'Dangerous Bridge Drive Slowly' instruction on the road sign (left) refers to the railway bridge on Ravenoak Road. The photograph, dated 1895, is taken from just past the junction with Swann Lane. The former surface of setts can be clearly seen. A commemorative stone on the present bridge records its widening by Cheadle and Gatley Urban District Council in 1934-35. Ravenoak Road, formerly Ravenoak Lane, was earlier called Pump Lane, from Pump Farm then nearby.

40. All Saints Church

The Jonathan Robinson School had been licensed for Divine Service on 10 November 1861. The foundation stone for the church was laid on 21 June 1862; it was consecrated on 12 August 1863 by the Bishop of Chester, Dr. John Graham. It was enlarged in 1878 to seat 580 people and further enlarged in 1898-99. The first Vicar was the Rev. J.H.D. Cochrane (1863-77). The church, paid for by public subscription, cost £1750; the architects were Medland and Henry Taylor. Pevsner says that it is "uninteresting outside, but that inside there is at least one oddity - the west and east termination of the arcades". Cheadle Hulme became a separate parish in 1868. After Bramall Hall was sold by the Davenport family, the bodies of three members of that family, interred in the vaults in the Hall's Chapel, were removed in the same year (1877) and were re-interred in All Saints' churchyard with their tombstones.

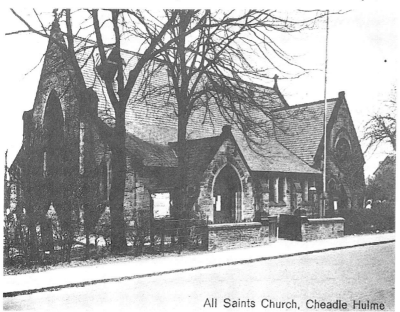

All Saints Church, Cheadle Hulme

41. All Saints Church
As may be seen in the drawing the church originally had a spire. A severe gale on 21/22 December 1894 blew the spire down, and it was never replaced.

42. All Saints Church

This view of the interior of the church comes from a coloured postcard sent in 1913 by M.J.Jones, Earlsdene, Cheadle Hulme, to Miss Evans, Police Station, Penhelig, Aberdovey. "It's always full on Sunday evenings". Would that it were so today!

INTERIOR OF ALL SAINTS, CHEADLE HULME

43. All Saints Church

This unusual view of the east end of the church (possibly taken from the Vicarage?) also shows the rural aspect of the village a century ago. The photograph dates prior to 1894 as the spire still exists; after it fell down, it was later replaced by a bell tower.

44. 'The Cottage' and Higham Street

The oldest part, overlooking the cobbled yard known as Higham Street (on the right of the photograph) is of sixteenth century origin - one source says it was built in 1539 - and is set on a plinth of local sandstone. For many years these properties were under threat of demolition due to intended road widening, a scheme now thankfully abandoned. 'The Cottage' was formerly reputedly an inn called *The Fox and Grapes*, and was later a farm and then a weaver's cottage. The local market was believed to have been held in the yard.

When the property was put up for sale in 1977 it was described as being "a fine example of Cheshire half-timbered construction with typical

The Cottage, Cheadle Hulme

black and white elevation with a stone roof. The part facing the garden is early-nineteenth century with large sash windows and louvred shutters under a slate roof. The whole has a 190ft frontage to Hulme Hall Road". The nineteenth century addition is actually called 'The old farmhouse' and has a garden of about three-quarters of an acre in extent. In recent years it has been enclosed by a high wall.

This area has changed but little; the photograph could have been taken any time from about 1910 to the1930s or later. I am told that it actually dates from 1928.

45. Hulme Hall

Hulme Hall was the manor house of the Vernon family and was later a home for Sir Edward Mosley. In 1867 it was bought by Isaac Storey, who, when undertaking alterations, found a lintel inscribed 'H D K 1419'. This may refer to a branch of the Kelsall family who owned Bradshaw Hall. A stone on that building, now demolished, was inscribed 'J K 1550', probably James Kelsall, buried at Cheadle on 11 April 1565. This illustration of Hulme Hall is taken from volume 2 (1892) of Heginbotham's *Stockport: ancient and modern.*

46. Hulme Hall

The Hall has been a home for the elderly for more than 40 years. This view is taken from a postcard sent in 1907.

Hulme Hall, Cheadle Hulme.

47. Church Road

This view comes from a postcard sent from Cheadle Hulme on 16 May 1906. What looks like an inscription round the porch of All Saints is actually ornamental stonework; in fact there is an inscription, but it is cut into the bevel-edge below the ornamental work. It reads: 'Enter into his gates with thanksgiving and into his courts with praise'. The National School is mainly hidden behind the trees, but a part of it can just be seen past the two figures in the centre. Church Road was previously Church Lane.

CHURCH ROAD, CHEADLE, HULME.

48. Hesketh Arms

The *Hesketh Arms* on Hulme Hall Road, seen here in 1895, was erected some time between 1864 and 1871 by William Bamford Hesketh, to replace the village inn called *The Horse and Jockey*. The old manor court - the Court Baron - continued to be held here until the early part of this century. Nineteenth-century licensees have been James Ford (1850) and Mrs. Betty Ford (1857 and 1864), W. Hooley, innkeeper and farmer (1872) and Mrs. Elizabeth Sooley (1878). In 1861, Mrs. Ford described herself as a 'farmer of 10 acres and publican'. She was then a 70 year-old widow and came from Withington. Her son-in-law, William Pell, was a railway parcel porter.

49. Joshua Brookes

The Rev. Joshua Brookes, commonly called 'Jotty' Brookes, was born in Cheadle Hulme in 1754 and baptised at Stockport on 19 May. His father, Thomas, a cripple, was a shoemaker or cobbler, and has been described as 'of uncouth mien, eccentric manners, and a great violence of temper'. Some of these qualities rubbed off on Joshua, who was known far and wide for his eccentricities and occasional violence, or certainly argumentative behaviour and rough manner. In 1771, Joshua took his M.A. at Brasenose College, Oxford, and from 1799 until his death in 1821, he was a chaplain at the Collegiate Church of Manchester (now the Cathedral, from 1847), a church he loved. A sympathetic portrait of Joshua may be found in *The Manchester Man* by Mrs. Linnaeus Banks.

50. Joseph Nadin

Born in 1765 at Fairfield, Derbyshire, he was a cotton spinner at Stockport before becoming Deputy Constable of Manchester in 1801. Whatever his other qualities, Nadin was a zealous, able, courageous and very thorough officer. He came to national prominence on 16 August 1819 when the Manchester magistrates ordered their Deputy Constable to arrest the leaders of the gathering in St. Peter's Fields. In minutes, 11 were dead and several hundred wounded at what was known forever afterwards as the Peterloo Massacre.

Nadin retired in 1821, to an estate he had purchased in Cheadle Hulme. His farm was situated about the area of the present Orrishmere Road. According to the 1844 Tithe Award he had just over 179 acres for which he paid the Rector of Cheadle £10. 5s. 5d. in rent; he also rented about three acres from Lloyd Bamford Hesketh Bamford, and about two acres from the Trustees of Dorothy Bulkeley's Charity. Nadin died in 1848 aged 83. He was a churchwarden at Cheadle Parish Church though he was buried at St.James's, Charlotte Street, Manchester; some of his descendants are buried at Cheadle.

JOSEPH NADIN
Deputy Constable of Manchester

51. Hilltop Farm

The original Hill Top (or Hilltop) Farm, near the junction of Hill Top Avenue and Swann Lane, is seen here *c.*1900. It has since been demolished, but some of its outbuildings were renovated to form the present residence of the same name. More recently it was the home of the BBC personality Brian Redhead and his family.

Hilltop Farm, Cheadle Hulme.

52. A 1942 drawing of Hilltop Farm

HILLTOP FARM 1942

53. Pinfold Farm

This was originally a one-up and one-down cottage, possibly dating from the eighteenth but perhaps more certainly from the nineteenth century, to which was added a barn, with a Dutch barn at the end. It ceased to be a working farm about 1930 when the surrounding farmland was sold and houses built. It is seen here *c.*1918. In the cottages across Hulme Hall Road was a blacksmith. Daniel Henshaw was in business at no.19 by 1906 and continued for several decades.

54. Pinfold Farm
In this photograph, from 1955, the farm shows its previous pseudo black-and-white appreance.

55. Peace Day, 1919

At 10 a.m. on Saturday, 19 July 1919, the children of Cheadle Hulme assembled at Mellor Street and then processed to "a field in Church Road" for a united Thanksgiving Service to celebrate the successful outcome of the Great War, as World War I came to be called. The procession was led by the Cheshire Military Band and the officiating ministers were the Rev.H.Tyson (All Saints) and the Rev. P.Ineson (Wesleyan Pastor). The "field in Church Road" became the site of the former Woods Lane School, now Cheadle Hulme College (see no.13).

56. Peace Day, 1919

In the afternoon there was a Carnival Procession which paraded the district, the participants being dressed in gala costume, and there were 22 prizes to be won. Here we see some of the winners, but I have unfortunately not been able to identify them. At 5 p.m., 600 children had tea in the Parish Room, demobilised men were in the Mission Room and the old folk over 65 were in the National School room. Later there were field sports for those aged 6-15 with 40 prizes, while for the adults there was a concert and dancing. The celebrations concluded with a firework display and the singing of the National Anthem.

57. The Cenotaph

In common with thousands of other places, the people of Cheadle Hulme honoured those who died in World War I by erecting a War Memorial. The site was one of three put before a subscriber's meeting in 1919 at which the Manor Road site received 46 votes, the Parish Room 13 and Ack Lane 9. The foundation stone was laid in 1920, the dedication ceremony on 2 June being presided over by the Rev. Henry Tyson, M.A., Vicar of All Saints, a position he had held since 1898. The procession to the site was led by the Styal Homes Band. Unfortunately, plans to complete the Memorial by Armistice Day, 11 November, were delayed. The architect wrote to the War Memorial Committee that "owing to the present disruption of industries, the futility of pressing for overtime operations, and the uncertainty of railway transit", he could not make any new arrangements. However by the following April it was "nearing completion, only lacking the figures of a soldier and a sailor".

58. The Cenotaph

The Dedication and Unveiling Service, "of a most impressive character", took place on Sunday, 29 May 1921, conducted by the Rev. Tyson. The Memorial was draped in the Union Jack prior to its unveiling, as we can see here. The service concluded with 'The Last Post' by two members from the Cheshire Regiment. The architect was Professor Beresford Pike, the figures are by Benjamin Clemens, masonry was by Messrs F.M. & H. Nuttall Ltd., Whitefield, and the bronze tablets were by Messrs John Morgan & Sons, London. The total cost, excluding the land, which was given gratuitously by the Directors of the Freehold Society, was £1300, raised by public subscription. The surmounting cross is of Rainhill stone - "a local material of pleasing colour" - and the site was laid out by members of the local branch of the Comrades of the Great War. This postcard view dates from shortly after the unveiling ceremony.

59. The Cenotaph
Also taken after the unveiling, this photograph shows more of the large crowd which attended this event.

60. The Cenotaph and Manor Road

I suspect that this was also taken at about the same time, but it is interesting as it shows the gates which used to stand across Manor Road. I don't know when they were removed but they were still there in 1958. Park Road disappears to the left.

61. Grove Lane Baptist Chapel

Grove Lane Baptist Chapel (actually on the corner of Pingate Lane and Chapel Walks) was built in 1840 and paid for by William Fowden, then aged 56, who was born in a nearby farmhouse. Fowden was concerned for the welfare of the people of this area. Not content with building the Chapel, he also paid for the Sunday School across the road on Grove Lane itself in 1846. For some years the Sunday School was also used as a Day School. Grove Lane Baptist Chapel was demolished in 1997 having been replaced by a smaller building nearby. The site is now a landscaped car park.

62. John Alcorn

John Alcorn was the first Pastor, taking up his duties in June 1840; he stayed for 21 years. Alcorn was a Scot and had been associated with Fowden and others at the Manchester City Mission, Grosvenor Street, where he was described as a man "of abounding vigour and glowing earnestness". Some idea of the fervour of this ardent young missionary - he was 21 or 22 on coming to Grove Lane - may be gathered by this extract from his diary:

'Sunday, preached at Grove Lane and superintended the Sunday School. Monday, Bible reading at the same place. Tuesday, preaching at Poynton. Wednesday, at Bollington. Thursday, at Alderley Edge.'

Alcorn was actively engaged in the progress and affairs of the village, and even served for a time as Chairman of the Highways Committee. The Baptist Divine, Dr.Clifford, wrote of Alcorn: "He was a preacher of the good news of salvation through Jesus Christ. This was his life-task. And those who remember his manly form, fervid style, and glowing eloquence, and have felt the thrill of his kindling personality, will be increasingly indebted unto him for his teaching and faithful ministry". This photograph of Alcorn dates from about 1880 when he was a little over 60 years of age.

63. Cross Roads

Not so much the cross roads, but rather a T-junction, in this case of Church Road (left) and Ack Lane (behind the photographer) with Ravenoak Road to the right, the sign directing travellers to Cheadle and Stockport. The black and white portion of the Vicarage (of All Saints) was taken down some years ago. The *Church Inn* then, as now, gives the appearance of having once perhaps been a cottage.

The delivery van belongs to J[ames] H[enry] Bennett, provision merchant, though directories only describe him as a grocer. In 1906 he lived in Oak Avenue, later moving to Hill Top Avenue. In 1910 he was at 16 Mellor Street; this had changed to Mellor Road by 1914, and he can be traced in directories at that address until at least 1938.

64. Dr.Edmondson's house

Dr.Edmondson, a well-known local doctor, lived here on Station Road. He became organist of the Congregational Church (see no.36) in 1936, a post he held for 32 years. After retiring from medical practice in 1963, he went to live at Llandudno, but for five years drove from Llandudno to Cheadle Hulme each Sunday for services, sometimes even coming during the week. The photograph was taken on 18 March 1962 just prior to the demolition of the house, to make way for the shopping precinct which opened later that year, and which has recently been modernised and refurbished.

65. The Nurseries

The Horticultural Company was formed in 1886 and during the 1920s and 1930s was run by Mr.J.Looker. Described as "nurserymen", the Company survived until the war period; their grounds are now a housing estate. This view is from a postcard sent in 1905 which acknowledges an order from Mr.Herbert Nicholson, Caverswall Road, Blythe Bridge, Stoke-on-Trent.

66. Nursery Road in 1956 with Heathbank Road in the distance

67. Higher Bent Farm

Both Higher Bent Farm, which stood in Gill Bent Road, and Lower Bent Farm, which still stands next to *The Smithy* public house, have associa-

tions with the Leather family, who have been in Cheadle Hulme for over 150 years. In 1844, Joseph Leather rented 75 acres from Thomas Taylor, while in 1887, David and John Leather were farming at Lower Bent Farm. By 1906, John Leather was at Higher Bent Farm, David was at Lower Bent Farm, and David junior was at Ladybridge Farm. In the last century the farms were known as Higher Bent House and Lower Bent House. Higher Bent Farm, seen here in 1955, has since been demolished. It carried an inscription 'T R C 1768'.

68. Stringer's Farm

Stringer's farm is not separately identified in directories until 1871 when the tenant was Mrs Martha Hooley; she is listed under 'farmers' as early as 1864. The name Stringer appears on a plan of Gill Bent in 1812 but is not found on the Tithe Map of 1844. This shows that two of the largest farmers in the area were the Hooleys and the Davenports. The Hooleys, John senior and John junior, had 122 acres between them, while the Dav-enports, George and John, had 91 acres. Mrs. Martha Hooley may be the widow of the John Hooley who farmed the land in 1844; the 1871 census shows that her daughter Mary was married to James Davenport, who in 1881 is shown as farming 23 acres. The barn of Stringer's Farm abutted onto the road, as seen in this photograph *c.*1910 which also shows part of the old farmhouse, believed to have dated from the 1780s.

69. First Methodist Chapel

We have already noted (see no.32) that a Methodist Sunday school existed at Lane End from 1814. Though there were Methodist Societies at Cheadle Hulme, Lane End and Smithy Green from 1787, only Lane End had a Sunday School, and Methodism in Cheadle Hulme has subsequently been concentrated in that area. The first purpose-built Methodist Chapel, seen here, was provided by Mr. James Leech of Stockport and a landowner in Cheadle Hulme. It opened in 1824 and was in use until 1884 when it was vacated (see no. 71), after which the premises were converted into dwelling houses named Wesley Terrace. These were demolished in January 1967 to make way for the widening of Station Road.

70. Chapel interior

The entrance to this first Chapel was reached by a flight of stone steps, for underneath the Chapel were four cottages or 'flats'. The interior of the Chapel, seen here, consisted of a gallery around the walls, the front wall accommodating the organ and choir. The organ had two manuals and was in a mahogony case surmounted by a cherub.

71. Second Methodist Chapel

The second Chapel and Schoolroom was built at the junction of Belfield Avenue and Station Road on land leased from the Brocklehurst family of Macclesfield (some of whose land had earlier been in Mr.Leech's estate). The Chapel was to seat 320, and the Schoolroom would hold about 200 scholars. The architect was Joseph Whittington; his name is given as John S.Whittington in the 1881 Census, aged 43, and he was listed as master-in-charge at Bramall Hall. The contractor was Mr R.Whittell of Blackley, Manchester. The Memorial Stone was laid on 14 July 1883 and the premises were officially opened for Divine Worship on 27 March 1884. The total cost was £2740. An unusual feature, and clearly seen in this photograph, about 1906, was the front with its gable incorporating a rose window. Another unusual feature was the rear in the form of an octagon or apse. On the night of 26/27 February 1963, the chapel was destroyed by fire though the registers and other documents were saved. The present, third, chapel on the corner of Ramillies Avenue and Station Road opened in 1968.

72. Cheadle Hulme Rangers

Described in the press as the Cheadle Hulme 'skid-kids' the cycle speedway team are seen here, in 1951, with their skipper, Lew Grepp (centre, on the bicycle). Lew had recently won the coveted golden helmet as All-England cycle speedway champion. Others in the photograph are, from the left: George Tomlinson, Dewi Williams, Frank Hayes, Jack Elliott, Brian Little, Doug Taylor and Bill Green.

73. Cheadle Hulme Rangers - League Champions

 Two years earlier, on Sunday, 16 October 1949, and the league champions pose for the camera. They are: Derek Maynard, Bill Green, Lew Grepp (on the bike), J.Bagley, Jack Elliott, Ken Stanley and Doug Taylor, with Ken Hutchinson and Jack Smith kneeling.

74. Carnival?

This is such an interesting and delightful photograph that I cannot resist including it. I haven't been able to positively identify the occasion; it's said to date from around 1909 but I wonder if that should be 1919, in which case it might show part of the carnival festivities on Peace Day (see pictures 55 and 56).

75-76. Stanley Hall

Over the doorway to Stanley Hall is the inscription 'John Brown 1662'. Whether this indicates that he built the Hall in that year, or whether he re-built an existing property, is uncertain. What is certain, however, is that in 1786, the Quakers' Cheshire Monthly Meeting bought the Stanley Green estate, consisting of farm buildings and 52 acres, from Elizabeth Mulliner for £1200. In 1838, just over 4 acres of the original Stanley Hall estate was sold to the Manchester and Birmingham Railway Company for their new line. The Stanley Green estate was finally sold by the Quakers in 1922.

77-78. Stanley Hall

The Hall had been in a dilapidated state for some time when the new owner undertook restoration work in 1974-75. The first three photographs, no.'s 75-77, show restoration work in progress, while the final one shows the Hall after restoration, in July 1976.

79-80. Park Garage, Station Road

Harry E. Madders left the Drakeson Motor Company (a part of Hollingdrake's) to set up on his own in November 1928. He bought Park Garage - an old army hut - on Station Road, which he set about modernising.

Photograph no.79 shows Park Garage in 1928; the workshop and lock-ups as in 1933 are seen in photograph no.80.

81. Park Garage, c.1935

His son Stuart, after completing an apprenticeship at Leyland Motors, eventually joined his father in January 1955. The firm had a Morris Motors dealership from 1931 to 1984 and is now a Peugeot specialist dealer. Their business is now concentrated at Unity Garage, the former Joseph Burrows & Son dealership, on Ack Lane West.

82. C.H.A.D.S.

Cheadle Hulme Amateur Dramatic Society was founded in 1921 and developed from the drama section of the Cheadle Hulme Cricket, Bowling and Tennis Club. Early productions were held in the Parish Hall and *Elysian Cinema*. In 1956 the present site was purchased and the new theatre was opened on Tuesday, 20 October 1959 with a production of Jean Anouilh's play *Dinner with the Family*. The opening ceremony was performed by the playwright Dr.L.du Garde Peach.

This first play in the new theatre, seen here in 1959, was the company's 96th production and was described by critics as "an artistic success" which had received "sparkling treatment".

Since 1959, continued expansion has seen the addition of a stage cyclorama, permanent backstage facilities, and a permanent, raked auditorium. Further improvements have also recently been completed. Over the years the company has won many awards, as have several of the individual players.

83. *Dinner with the Family*

The full cast of *Dinner with the Family* is seen here and consisted of Edna Peel, David Jordan, Kenneth Royds, James P. Barker, Onie Marsh, Sheila Wetherell, Leonard Simpson, Desmond Clements, Peggy Ducklin, Betty Heap and Joan Jordan. The decor was by Reginald Dixon and the producer was Charles Bury.

84. *The Living Room*

The earliest photographs in the company's collection date from March 1946, when their 56th production, *The Living Room* by Esther McCracken was mounted, also produced by Charles Bury. Here is a scene from that production.

85. Cheadle Hulme Cricket Club

In 1892 the Manchester and District Cricket Association was founded, to which the Cheadle Hulme Cricket Club, founded in 1881, was admitted in 1893. This began an 82-year connection which ended in 1975, when the Club became one of the founder-members of the Cheshire County League. This is the earliest known photograph of a Cheadle Hulme Club cricket team and it was probably taken between 1898 and 1902.

According to the 1981 centenary brochure, the gentlemen are:
Back Row: H. Teacher (Pro.), H. Royle, A. Cadman, J. Rome (President), E. Rome, A. Squires (Umpire), E. Radford, A.Rome.
Middle Row (only two of the three are identified): A. Taylor, G.E. Haworth (Captain 1898-1903 and later), and A.N. Other.
Front Row: W. Stokes (Scorer), P. Mason, C. Williams, C. Rome (Wicket-keeper).
James Rome, the bearded gentleman in the back roe, was the father of the other Romes.

79

86. Cheadle Hulme Cricket Club

The Club's first playing field was adjacent to Mr.Leather's farm on Ladybridge Road and was leased from him. Improvements made over the years culminated in the opening of a new two-storey clubhouse in May 1939. Disaster struck in the early hours of 8 May 1946 when a fire reduced the clubhouse to a shell, as this *Manchester Evening News* photograph graphically records.

In 1967 Manchester Rugby [Union] Football Club sold its ground in Salford and transferred to Cheadle Hulme. The 22-acre Grove Park ground is shared jointly between these two Clubs. The Cricket Club has won many trophies, but they might prefer to forget that the first ball bowled at Grove Park was a wide!

87. Jubilee Street Party

Finally, while most of the photographs in a book of this kind are fifty or more years old, more recent events have now become 'history'. Here the residents of Malmesbury Road celebrate the Queen's Silver Jubilee with a street party in June 1977. The Hursthead Estate, as it was called when Messrs G. Wimpey developed the site in the late 1960s and early 1970s, was named after Hursthead Farm. Fletcher Moss, writing at the turn of the century, described the farm, originally timber-built, as "a very bleak and lonely place with no roads leading to it - only footpaths and a cart-track". Well, that's certainly changed!

88–89. Jubilee Street Party

Two more scenes from the Street Party. There were races for the children and the residents of Malmesbury Road enjoyed a buffet meal. Similar events took place elsewhere.

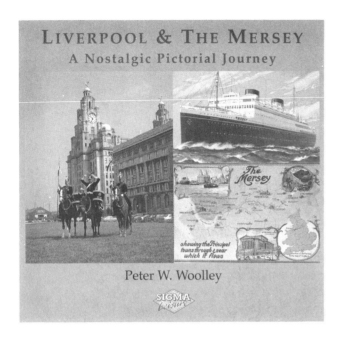

LIVERPOOL & THE MERSEY:
a nostalgic pictorial journey

Peter Woolley

This nostalgic trip begins at Liverpool city centre, carries on through the suburbs to Transporter Bridge at Runcorn, and comes to an end along the Mersey and the docks to New Brighton. Transport, shipping, splendid old buildings and social commentary intermingle in this delightful collection of rare city scenes.

£8.95

Our books are all available through bookshops. In case of difficulty, or for a free catalogue, please contact:
SIGMA LEISURE, 1 SOUTH OAK LANE, WILMSLOW, CHESHIRE SK9 6AR. *Phone: 01625-531035; Fax: 01625-536800.*
E-mail: sigma.press@zetnet.co.uk . Web site: http//www.sigmapress.co.uk
Credit card orders welcome. Please add £2 p&p to all orders.